FOCUS ON ELEMENTARY

Laboratory Workbook

Rebecca W. Keller, PhD

Illustrations: Janet Moneymaker

Focus On Elementary Astronomy Laboratory Workbook
ISBN 978-1-936114-45-0

Published by Gravitas Publications, Inc.
www.gravitaspublications.com

Printed in United States

A Note From the Author

Hi!

In this curriculum you are going to learn the first step of the scientific method:

Making good observations!

In astronomy making good observations is very important.

Each experiment in this workbook is divided into several different sections. There is a section called *Observe It* where you will make observations. In the *Think About It* section you will answer questions., and in the *What Did You Discover?* section you will write down or draw what you observed in the experiment. There is a section called *Why?* where you will learn about why you may have observed certain things. And finally, there is a section called *Just For Fun* that has an extra activity for you to experiment with.

These experiments will help you learn the first step of the scientific method and . . . they're lots of fun!

Enjoy!

Rebecca W. Keller, PhD

Contents

Experiment 1

Twinkle, Twinkle Little Star

I. Observe It

❶ On a clear night, go outside and look up at the sky to see the stars. Take a moment to adjust your eyes so you can see the stars well, and just observe.

❷ In the space below draw what you see.

❸ Try to find the largest star. Draw below.

❹ Try to find the brightest star. Draw below.

❺ Try to find a twinkling star. Draw below.

❻ Try to find stars of different colors. Draw below.

II. Think About It

❶ Do you think the largest star is also the brightest star? Why or why not?

_____

_____

_____

_____

❷ Do you think all of the "stars" are stars? Could some of them be planets? Why or why not?

_____

_____

_____

_____

❸ Do you think the brightest star is the closest star? Why or why not?

_____

_____

_____

_____

III. What Did You Discover?

❶ How many stars could you find? Could you draw them all?

_____

_____

❷ Which star was the brightest star?

_____

_____

❸ Was the brightest star the largest star?

_____

_____

❹ Were any of the stars twinkling?

_____

_____

❺ Why do you think stars twinkle?

_____

_____

IV. Why?

The night sky is full of stars. No matter where you live, on a clear night you can see stars. As you go farther away from city lights, you can see even more stars.

Not all stars look the same. Some stars are brighter than other stars, some stars are larger than other stars, and some stars twinkle. Stars are not all the same color. Some stars look red, some white, and some blue. The colors of stars can be very hard to see without a telescope.

Not all of the "stars" that we see in the sky are actually stars. Some of them are planets. Planets don't make their own light like stars do, but planets look like stars because, like a mirror, they reflect the Sun's light. This makes them look like stars to our eyes. Sometimes the brightest "star" is a planet!

V. Just For Fun

See if you can find some stars that are twinkling. To really see the stars it is important to be patient, sit still, and just observe. You can learn a great deal about stars just by looking at them.

If you are patient enough, you might see some stars twinkle. The air you are looking through to see the stars contains small particles that are moving around, and this can make the stars look like they are twinkling. However, sometimes a star really is changing its brightness. This might be a nova or supernova!

The earliest astronomers used just their eyes to observe the stars. Observing stars is the first step towards knowing about them!

Experiment 2

Building a Telescope

I. Observe It

❶ Take the sheet of heavy paper, roll it into a tube and tape it together. Next, carefully examine all of the pieces of the telescope.

❷ Which parts are the lenses? How can you tell?

_____

_____

_____

❸ How many tubes are there?

_____

❹ What do you think the different tubes do?

_____

_____

_____

❺ How far do you think you will be able to see with your telescope?

_____

_____

_____

II. Think About It

Assemble and experiment with the telescope.

❶ Take the eyepiece lens and the tube that you made from the heavy paper. Adjust the tube so that it fits around the eyepiece lens. Carefully tape the edges of the lens to the tube. Try not to cover too much of the lens with tape.

❷ Tape the other lens (the objective lens) carefully to one end of the paper towel tube. Again, try not to cover too much of the lens with tape.

❸ Slide the open end of the heavy paper tube that has the eyepiece lens into the open end of the paper towel tube. Your telescope is now ready to use.

❹ In the daylight look at a faraway object with your eyes, then through the telescope. Does the object look different through the telescope?

   Try sliding the tube in and out and observe what happens. Does what you are seeing change?

❺ In the daylight observe several different faraway objects, first with only your eyes and then with your telescope. In the spaces provided, draw what you see.

Eyes Only	Telescope

Eyes Only	Telescope

Eyes Only	Telescope

❻ In the evening, once the Sun has set and you can see stars, use your telescope to observe several stars. Draw or describe what you observe. Remember to be patient and make careful observations.

Object 1

Object 2

Object 3

Object 4

Object 5

Object 6

III. What Did You Discover?

❶ How easy or difficult was it to assemble the telescope?

_____

_____

_____

❷ How well did your telescope work?

_____

_____

_____

❸ Were you able to see more details of objects when you used your telescope than with your eyes only?

_____

_____

_____

❹ What features of stars were you able to observe that you couldn't observe with your eyes only?

_____

_____

_____

IV. Why?

Telescopes are tools that make faraway objects appear closer. Astronomers use telescopes to see faraway planets and stars. A basic telescope is easy to assemble and only requires two lenses and a long tube.

By comparing what you see when using only your eyes to what you can see with your telescope, you can better understand just how much a telescope helps astronomers see faraway objects. Part of learning how to make good observations is knowing what something looks like with and without the use of an instrument or tool, such as a telescope. With good observation skills you can see details in the Moon and stars that you might otherwise not notice.

V. Just For Fun

Hold a basketball and carefully observe it. What features can you notice?

Now place the basketball far away and look at it with only your eyes. What features can you see now?

Leaving the basketball in the same place, look at it through your telescope. What features can you see with the telescope that you couldn't see when you used only your eyes?

Try this experiment with the basketball placed at different distances away. You can also try it with other objects. Note your observations below or on a separate piece of paper.

NOTES

Experiment 3

Earth, Moon, and Sun

I. Observe It

❶ Cut out the continents on the following page.

❷ Glue or tape the continents onto a large basketball with North America, South America, and Greenland on one side; and Australia, Africa, Europe, Russia, and Asia on the other side.

❸ Cut a 2.5 centimeter (one inch) wide piece from the end of a toilet paper cylinder. This will give you a nice ring to place the basketball on. When you place the basketball on this cardboard ring, tilt the ball slightly off-center.

❹ Walk several feet away from the basketball, and turning off the room lights, shine a flashlight on the basketball.

❺ Leaving the flashlight shining on the basketball, rotate the basketball counterclockwise. Record your observations below.

_____

_____

_____

_____

_____

_____

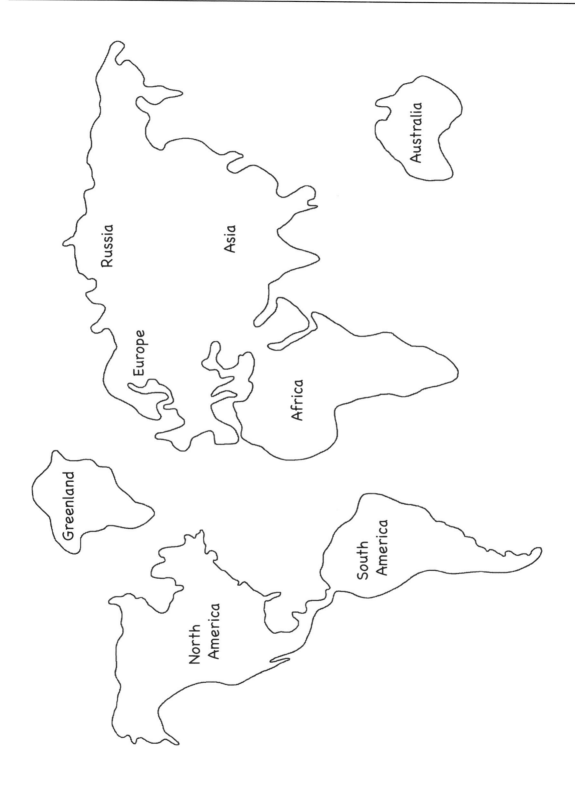

❻ Take the ping-pong ball, and holding it a short distance away from the basketball, move the ping-pong ball in a counterclockwise circle around the basketball. Record your observations below.

_____

_____

_____

_____

_____

II. Think About It

❶ Can you determine how day and night are created by the rotation of Earth?

_____

_____

_____

_____

❷ Can you observe how a lunar eclipse forms (where Earth casts a shadow on the Moon)?

_____

_____

_____

❸ Can you observe how a solar eclipse forms (where the Moon casts a shadow on Earth)?

_____

_____

_____

_____

❹ Using the basketball and flashlight, can you model the seasons? Explain how you would do this.

_____

_____

_____

III. What Did You Discover?

❶ Explain how day and night occur.

_____

_____

_____

❷ Explain how a lunar eclipse occurs.

_____

_____

_____

❸ Explain how a solar eclipse occurs.

_____

_____

_____

❹ What causes the different seasons?

_____

_____

_____

IV. Why?

In this experiment you observed what happens when the Sun shines on the Earth and the Moon. In this experiment the Sun is represented by the flashlight, Earth is represented by the basketball, and the Moon is represented by the ping-pong ball.

When you rotated the basketball (Earth), the flashlight (Sun) was shining on different parts of the ball. This action, (the Sun shining on a rotating Earth) is what causes night and day.

When you took the ping-pong ball (Moon) and rotated it around the basketball (Earth), you observed how the Moon casts a shadow on Earth when the Moon is between the Sun and the Earth. You also observed how the Earth casts a shadow on the Moon when the Earth is between the Sun and the Moon. These illustrate solar and lunar eclipses.

You also found out how seasons occur. The Earth's tilt causes the seasons. As the Earth circles the Sun, some parts of Earth tilt towards the Sun and some parts tilt away. This tilting of the Earth creates seasons.

V. Just For Fun

Think about what would be different if the Earth's axis pointed directly at the Sun. Would this change the seasons where you live? Would it change night and day?

Now think about what it would be like if the Earth's axis went through the equator instead of going through the North and South Poles. Would this change the seasons? Would it change night and day?

Try using the basketball and the flashlight to experiment with these ideas.

Seeing the Moon

I. Observe It

❶ For fourteen days, observe the Moon at night. Notice any details about how it appears to you.

❷ Record your observations. Note the color and shape.

1	2
3	4

5

6

7

8

9

10

11

12

13

14

II. Think About It

❶ Does the color of the Moon stay the same or change?

_____

_____

_____

❷ Does the shape of the Moon stay the same or change?

_____

_____

_____

❸ What do you find most interesting about the Moon?

_____

_____

_____

_____

_____

_____

III. What Did You Discover?

❶ Why does the shape of the Moon change?

_____

_____

_____

❷ Where does the Moon get its light?

_____

_____

_____

❸ Do you think the Moon actually changes shape, or does it just look like it has changed shape because the Sun shines on different parts of the Moon on different days?

_____

_____

_____

_____

_____

IV. Why?

In this experiment you observed the shape and color of the Moon for several days. As the Moon circles the Earth, the shape of the Moon appears to change. Depending on when you began observing the Moon, you may have seen a full Moon (completely round), a half Moon (half-round), or a crescent Moon (a curved shape).

As the Moon circles the Earth, the Sun illuminates different sections of the part of the Moon that faces us. This makes the shape of the Moon appear to change as we view it from Earth.

Since it takes almost one month for the Moon to circle the Earth, the Moon will cycle through the different shapes each month. The Moon will go from full Moon, to half Moon, to new (dark) Moon, back to half Moon, and then the cycle will begin again.

V. Just For Fun

In the evening find the Moon in the sky and observe it carefully. What details do you notice? What shape is it? Is it a full Moon? Is it a half Moon? Does it look like there's a face on the Moon? Draw and color the Moon as you see it or as you imagine it.

Experiment 5

Modeling the Planets

I. Observe It

❶ In this experiment you will explore building models of the planets. Building models is important because it gives scientists a way to help them think about things that they cannot observe close up.

❷ Look at the illustrations of the planets in Chapter 5 of the student textbook. Note the sizes and colors of the eight planets. Make notes about what you observe.

_____

_____

_____

_____

_____

_____

_____

❸ Take the eight styrofoam balls and assign a styrofoam ball to represent each planet.

❹ Using the information you've collected, paint each styrofoam ball to look like the planet it represents.

II. Think About It

❶ How did you decide which styrofoam ball to assign to Jupiter?

_____

_____

_____

❷ How did you decide which styrofoam ball to assign to Mercury?

_____

_____

_____

❸ Did you notice any similarities or differences between any of the planets?

_____

_____

_____

III. What Did You Discover?

❶ What did building models of the planets help you to observe?

_____

_____

_____

❷ What features did you notice that make the planets different from each other?

_____

_____

_____

❸ How easy or difficult was it to model the planets?

_____

_____

_____

_____

_____

IV. Why?

In this experiment you explored building models to help you understand more about Earth and the other seven planets that orbit the Sun. Since scientists are not able to go to each of the planets, they use tools to make observations. Then, based on their observations, the scientists make models that show what they think the planets are like.

Models may not be accurate, but they are a scientist's best guess based on the information available. Sometimes using a model will lead a scientist to ask more questions. The answers may add to the scientist's knowledge and can result in changes to the model that make it more accurate.

Scientists can also make mental models of ideas that they have about how things work or why things are the way they are. These mental models may be written in words or pictures or explained with mathematics, and they can lead to many new discoveries.

V. Just For Fun

Think of some other things you could use to build models of the planets. Maybe you could find fruits of different sizes to be the planets. Are there vegetables that would work? Candies? Could you use a mixture of different kinds of items?

See if you can invent some different ways to model the planets.

Experiment 6

Modeling an Orbit

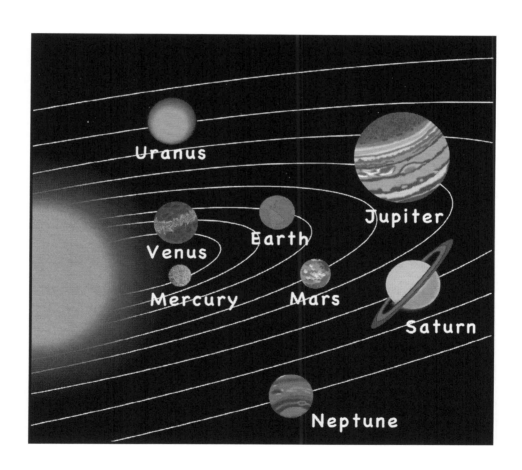

I. Think About It

In this experiment you will use a styrofoam ball attached to a string. While holding the end of the string, you will whirl the ball around in a circle. Before you do the experiment think about what might happen.

❶ What do you think will happen when you hold the end of the string and whirl the ball?

_____

_____

❷ Do you think the ball will fall towards your hand when you whirl it?

_____

_____

❸ Do you think the ball will fly off the end of the string when you whirl it?

_____

_____

❹ If you shorten the string, do you think the ball will move faster or slower?

_____

_____

II. Observe It

❶ Take a styrofoam ball, and with the help of an adult, punch a hole through the center.

❷ Next, create a large knot at one end of a piece of string. Thread the unknotted end of the string through the hole in the styrofoam ball, and pull the string through the ball until you have enough string to hold in your hand. The end of the string that has the knot will hang down from the other side of the ball.

❸ Hold the unknotted end of the string. The ball should be near your hand. Whirl the string until the styrofoam ball is moving in a circle with your hand at the center. Observe how the ball moves. In the space below, draw or write about what you see.

❹ Shorten the length of the string by holding it in the middle. The ball will be next to the knot. Repeat Step 3. Observe how the ball moves. In the space below, draw or write what you see.

❺ Shorten the length of the string again, this time holding it close to the styrofoam ball. Repeat Step 3. Observe how the ball moves. In the space below, draw or write what you see.

III. What Did You Discover?

❶ How easy or difficult was it to use the string to whirl the ball in a circle?

_____

_____

_____

❷ As you were whirling the ball, did it keep moving on a straight path or did it orbit around your hand?

_____

_____

_____

❸ What happened when you shortened the string? Did the ball move slower or faster?

_____

_____

_____

❹ Was it easier or more difficult to whirl the ball with a shorter string? Why?

_____

_____

_____

IV. Why?

When you started whirling the ball, it was near your hand. The whirling motion of the string caused the ball to travel in a circle around your hand and to slide along the string. The ball moved outward away from your hand until it was stopped by the knot. At this point the string was pulling the ball inward toward your hand, and the motion of the ball was pulling it outward, away from your hand. The pulling inward and the pulling outward are different types of force. Once the ball had traveled down the string as far as it could, the inward and outward forces were balanced, and the ball kept traveling in a circular orbit at the same distance from your hand.

The planets move in their orbits around the Sun in much the same way. The Sun's gravity pulls a planet toward it. At the same time, the momentum, or force, of the planet's motion pulls it outward. Because these forces are balanced, each planet stays in a near circular orbit around the Sun.

V. Just For Fun

Place a marble in an empty cup. Now move the cup around in a circle so that the marble travels around the inner surface of the cup. Start moving the cup slowly and then gradually move it faster. What happens as you change the speed? What happens when you move the cup really slowly? What happens if you move the cup in a circle really fast?

Try repeating this experiment using different size marbles and different size cups. Does changing the sizes change your results?

Experiment 7

Brightest or Closest?

OUR SUN   PROXIMA CENTAURI   ALPHA CENTAURI A   ALPHA CENTAURI B

I. Think About It

In this experiment you will observe two sources of
light—a flashlight and a glow stick.

❶ Which do you think will give off more light—the
flashlight or the glow stick?

_____

_____

❷ Do you think the glow stick or the flashlight will
illuminate a path the farthest?

_____

_____

❸ Do you think the flashlight or the glow stick would be
easier to see from far away?

_____

_____

❹ Would you use a flashlight or a glow stick to find your
way in a dark forest? Why?

_____

_____

II. Observe It

❶ Take the glow stick, and bending it gently, break the inner chamber so the two liquids in it mix and the glow stick lights up.

❷ On a dark night or in a dark room, use the glow stick to illuminate a path in front of you. In the space below record how far you can see.

❸ Take the flashlight and turn it on. Make sure the batteries are fresh.

❹ Repeat Step 2 with the flashlight. Observe how far you can see with the flashlight. Record your observations below.

❺ Place the shining glow stick and the lit flashlight side-by-side on the ground. Walk several meters (yards) away from them. Being careful not to look directly into the flashlight, observe whether you can see both the flashlight and the glow stick. Record your observations below.

❻ Return to the flashlight and glow stick that are sitting on the ground. Move the flashlight several meters (yards) farther away, behind the glow stick.

❼ Again walk several meters (yards) away from both. Being careful not to look directly into the flashlight, observe the glow stick and flashlight. Record your observations below.

III. What Did You Discover?

❶ Did the glow stick or the flashlight illuminate farther?

_____

_____

❷ With the glow stick and the flashlight side-by-side, could you see both clearly?

_____

_____

❸ What happened when you moved the flashlight behind the glow stick?

_____

_____

_____

❹ Did the glow stick look brighter than the flashlight when it was closer than the flashlight? Why or why not?

_____

_____

_____

IV. Why?

How brightly a star shines in the night sky has more to do with how much light energy the star gives out than how close the star is to Earth. A flashlight is able to product more light energy than a glow stick. You observed this by noticing that a flashlight will illuminate much farther along a path than a glow stick will.

When the glow stick and flashlight are observed from far away, the brightness of the flashlight can overwhelm and wash out the brightness of the glow stick even if the glow stick is closer than the flashlight. The same thing happens with stars. Stars that are brighter but farther away can wash out the light from stars that are less bright but closer. This can make it challenging for astronomers to see dim stars.

V. Just For Fun

Try the same experiment with different colored glow sticks and see if your results change. Does the color matter? Are some colors brighter than others?

Experiment 8

See the Milky Way

I. Think About It

In this experiment you will look at the Milky Way.

❶ Looking at the Milky Way is like looking at your city. If you are near the edge of your city and you can see tall buildings from where you are, look for the area that has the most tall buildings. This will probably be the center of your city. If you can see the center of your city, draw it below. If you can't actually see the center, draw what you think it might look like. If you don't live in a city, think about one you have visited or seen in movies or pictures, and draw what you think a city center looks like.

❷ When you look away from the center of the city you will probably see fewer buildings. If you can look away from the center of your city, draw what you see below. If you can't actually see away from the center or if you don't live in a city, draw what you think the part of the city that is farther away from the center might look like.

❸ Let the buildings in the center of your city represent stars in our galaxy. In the space below, draw what the stars in the center of our galaxy might look like.

❹ Letting the buildings that are farther away from the city center represent stars, draw what you think the stars that are farther away from the center of our galaxy might look like.

II. Observe It

❶ Find an area that is free of city lights on a clear night when there is no moon.

❷ Look into the night sky without a telescope or binoculars. Use only your eyes.

❸ Study the sky and observe areas where there are lots of stars. Compare this to areas with fewer stars.

❹ See if you can find a band of stars stretching across the night sky.

❺ In the space below, draw what you observe.

III. What Did You Discover?

❶ How many stars did you see?

_____

_____

❷ Were there areas with lots of stars and other areas with fewer stars?

_____

_____

❸ Were you able to see a band of stars stretching across the night sky?

_____

_____

❹ If you could see this band of stars, do you think you were seeing the center of the Milky Way or the edge of the Milky Way? Why or why not?

_____

_____

_____

IV. Why?

It's amazing to think that we can see a huge galaxy like our Milky Way, but it's possible. Earth is located at just the right spot in the galaxy that we can observe it. Also, Earth has an atmosphere that allows us to look through the air to see the stars.

When you see a band of stars stretching across the night sky, you are actually looking toward the center of the Milky Way Galaxy. Because the Milky Way is a flat, disk-shaped spiral and we are looking at it from the edge, the stars you observe as you look toward the center of the galaxy appear as a band of stars across the sky. If we lived closer to the center of the galaxy, we would see so many stars all around us that it would be difficult to know which way to look to see toward the center.

V. Just For Fun

If you have a computer and would like to see the Milky Way Galaxy, download Google Earth from the internet. Follow the setup instructions. Click on the planet symbol at the top, choose "Sky" from the drop down menu, and type "Milky Way" in the search box. What do you discover?

Experiment 9

How Do Galaxies Get Their Shapes?

I. Think About It

Galaxies are groups of stars, planets, comets, asteroids, and dust. All of these objects in space clump together and form particular shapes because of gravity. Gravity is the force that holds everything together in a galaxy.

Answer the following questions:

❶ How do you think galaxies form?

_____

_____

_____

_____

_____

❷ What do you think holds planets and stars together?

_____

_____

_____

_____

_____

❸ What do you think causes spiral galaxies?

_____

_____

_____

_____

_____

_____

_____

❹ What do you think causes irregular galaxies?

_____

_____

_____

_____

_____

_____

_____

II. Observe It

In this experiment you will simulate the force of gravity on stars and other objects in space by using a magnet to move small magnetic particles. Magnetic force is different from gravitational force but similar enough to use it to model galaxy formation.

❶ Take a shallow, flat-bottomed plastic container and pour corn syrup into it until it is just below the top.

❷ Add the iron filings with the help of an adult.

❸ Carefully cover the plastic container with plastic wrap.

❹ Place the magnets underneath the plastic container and observe the iron filings. Record your observations in the space below.

❺ Take one of the magnets and create a swirling pattern. Record your observations in the space below.

❻ Take both magnets and create opposite swirling patterns Record your observations below.

❼ Bring the two magnets together and observe what happens. Record your observations.

❽ Play with the magnets and iron filings. Try moving the magnets in different ways. Record your observations.

Magnet movement: _____

Observations

Magnet movement: _____

Observations

Magnet movement: _____

Observations

III. What Did You Discover?

❶ What happened to the iron filings when you placed the magnet below them?

_____

_____

_____

_____

_____

_____

❷ When you swirled the magnet, did spiral arms form? Was there a center?

_____

_____

_____

_____

_____

_____

❸ What happened when you brought the two magnets together and allowed the iron filings to follow?

_____

_____

_____

_____

_____

_____

❹ Were you able to create any irregular shapes? Describe below what you did.

_____

_____

_____

_____

_____

_____

IV. Why?

Galaxies form because the gravitational forces of stars pull on each other and on planets, comets, asteroids, ice, and dirt. When a force pulls on an object, the object will begin to move.

In this experiment you built a model using iron filings and magnets to observe what is possible when forces move objects. You were able to see how magnets pull on iron filings to create different shapes. In much the same way, stars pull on each other and on planets and other objects in space to create the shapes of galaxies.

V. Just For Fun

Make a Jell-O galaxy.

With the help of an adult, follow the instructions on a box of flavored gelatin. Add grapes, berries, or other fruits cut into small pieces. Before the gelatin cools, swirl the fruit into a spiral galaxy, bar galaxy, or irregular galaxy. How many different kinds of galaxies can you make?

Experiment 10

Making a Comet

I. Think About It

A comet is a mixture of dirt and ice. When a comet travels close enough to the Sun, the ice will vaporize, turning into gas. This gas then creates a tail that follows the comet as it moves through space.

❶ Draw what you think a comet might look like in space when it is far away from the Sun.

❷ Draw what you think a comet in space might look like as it gets close to the Sun.

II. Observe It

❶ Collect some dirt and small stones.

❷ Pour the dirt and stones into a small pail and cover with water. Do not fill to the top. Leave several inches between the water and the top of the pail.

❸ Place the pail in the freezer and allow the water to freeze.

❹ Tap the frozen mixture out of the pail.

❺ Observe the frozen mixture. In the space below, draw or write about what you see.

❻ Observe the mixture as it melts. Draw or write about your observations.

❼ Repeat Steps ❶-❹ using more water. Draw or write about your observations.

❽ Repeat Steps ❶-❹ using more dirt. Draw or write about your observations.

III. What Did You Discover?

❶ Do you think your frozen mixture of water, dirt, and rocks looks like a real comet? Why or why not?

_____

_____

_____

_____

❷ What happened as your comet melted? Did it come apart in chunks, or did it melt slowly?

_____

_____

_____

_____

❸ How quickly do you think your comet would come apart if it were near the Sun?

_____

_____

_____

_____

❹ How much ice do you think a comet would need to have for you to be able to see its tail from Earth?

_____

_____

_____

_____

❺ How much bigger than your comet model do you think a real comet is?

_____

_____

_____

_____

IV. Why?

In this experiment you modeled a comet. Comets are large chunks of ice and rock that move through space. A real comet would probably look very similar to the small comet model you made from ice, dirt, and rocks, but it would be much larger.

The ice in your comet model melted, but in a real comet the ice would vaporize, turning into gas without becoming a liquid first. Although the method by which the comet loses its ice is different in your experiment than it is for a real comet, this model lets you see what happens to a comet as it loses ice. It gets smaller and begins to break apart until the comet eventually disappears.

Scientists are not always able to make models that work exactly like the object they are modeling. But by making substitutions, scientists can still make valuable observations about objects they cannot get close to.

V. Just For Fun

With the help of an adult, make a water, dirt, and rock mixture and then add dry ice to it. How does the dry ice change your comet?

Made in the USA
Charleston, SC
05 December 2014